Mullet Madness!

Mullet Madness!

The Haircut That's Business Up Front and a Party in the Back

Alan Henderson

Skyhorse Publishing

www.skyhorsepublishing.com

Library of Congress Control Number: 2007936177

10 9 8 7 6 5 4 3 2 1

ISBN 13: 978-1-60239-113-0
ISBN 10: 1-60239-113-0

Book design by DILONÉ
Printed in the United States of America

Acknowledgments and Dedication

My thanks to my family, to the people who contributed to
this book, and to my friends at www.mulletjunky.com.
I dedicate this book to everyone who has ever worn a mullet.
Without you, and your sense of style, this book could not exist.

" Oh, I feel so delightfully white trash. Mommy, I want a mullet. "

— Stewie, *Family Guy*

Table of Contents

Chapter One   The Mullet—More Than a Hairstyle   8

Chapter Two   Mullet History, Lore, and Legend   20

Chapter Three   Famous Mullets   34

Chapter Four   How to Cut a Mullet   74

Chapter Five   A Field Guide to Mullets   82

Chapter Six   A Handy Mullet Reference Guide   114

Chapter One

The Mullet—
More Than a Hairstyle

" I attribute my success as an actor [in Thelma and Louise*] to my hair…. I believe that because of the mullet, director Ridley Scott was able to visualize me as the thief… Again, for* Legends *[of the Fall, 1994], even though I had grown the mullet out by then, I think it was because of my former mulletude that I was able to nab the role as a wife-stealing brother. "*

—Brad Pitt

We know which of these guys won't find a girl at this party—the guy without the mullet!

Mullet (mu' lit), n: any of a family (Mugilidae) of edible, spiny-rayed fishes found worldwide in fresh and salt coastal waters and having a small mouth and feeble teeth, as the striped (or gray) mullet. They are frequently seen grubbing about in the sand or mud for microscopic plants, small animals, and other food. Mullets have served as an important source of food in Mediterranean Europe since Roman times. It is one of the most commercially harvested species of fish in Florida. Their average weight is two to three pounds. Four ounces of mullet has 130 calories.

There are many books on catching and cooking the mullet. This isn't another one. *Mullet Madness!* is not about rampaging fish, but about the rampaging hairstyle that's "business in the front, party in the back." You know the 'do I'm talking about: think Billy Ray Cyrus and his achy breaky heart, think Patrick Swayze in *Road House.* In the 1980s, the mullet was sported by countless singers, athletes, and actors (and actresses). Today, mullets are a little harder to find, but they can still be found all over the world. The mullet may be an acquired taste,

A mullet: more than just a fish.

A timeless style—blue jeans, a white t-shirt, and a mullet.

but no one can argue that they are cleverly aerodynamic and functional. Some consider it a flattering hairstyle, allowing a man to have long hair, yet be able to look neat and well-groomed. With a mullet, he can let his freak flag fly, but by just pulling his hair back in a ponytail and tucking it under a collar he is ready for a meeting with a Fortune 500 CEO (maybe). Otherwise, he can let it just kick back and let the breeze blow through his long, luxurious hair.

The mullet is more than a haircut. It's a way of life, a state of mind, an attitude. With little or no maintenance, the mullet insulates the neck in the cold; on warm days, it can be tied into a ponytail or even braided. Mullet sightings often elicit strong responses, pro or con. It's a haircut remarkable for its ability to offend, intrigue, entertain, intrigue, startle, and even excite. Some find the mullet noble, handsome, even graceful. Others find it crude, low brow, or rebellious. It has spawned a plethora of varieties. Common varieties like the skullet (shaved on top, long in back) and the femullet (female mullet) can be spotted in almost every American city or town. Sightings of varieties like the mullhawk (part Mohawk, part mullet) and the frolet (part Afro, part mullet) are rare.

So which came first, the fish or the hair? The fish, clearly. But how did the name of this fairly ordinary fish attach itself to this extraordinary hairstyle? According to Icelandic fishing lore, the fishermen who took to the sea in pursuit of these fish typically grew their hair long in the back in order to keep warm and dry on blustery days. Perhaps their quarry gave its name to their haircut. Frankly, we may never know the real history of the name, but that story is as good as any.

In America, a "mullet head," probably in reference to the fish or possibly, in modern usage, as a reference to the haircut, is someone lacking in intelligence or common sense. Mark Twain used the term "mullet-head" in his classic of American literature, *Huckleberry Finn*, first published in 1885. Tom Sawyer says of his oblivious aunt and uncle: "They're so confiding and mullet-headed they don't take notice of nothing at all." Over eighty years later, the term was used again in the 1967 Paul Newman movie *Cool Hand Luke*. The character Dragline, played by George Kennedy (who won an Oscar for his role), scolds a fellow card player for losing a pot to Newman, who was bluffing: "Nothin'. A handful of nothin'. You stupid mullet head. He beat you with nothin'."

A handsome mullet, shades, a necklace, and an earring can make any man stylish.

The term "mullet head" is recorded in both the *Oxford English Dictionary* and the *Historical Dictionary of American Slang*, and various sources define it as meaning "fool," "blockhead," "numskull," or "foolish person." Knowing this definition, is it implied that those who favor the mullet hairstyle are blockheads, or fools? Is there a connection?

Perhaps the wordsmiths can provide the answer. Linguist

Like father, like son.

John Algeo notes a usage of the term "mull-head" in England to mean "a dull, stupid fellow," and he alleges a relationship with two senses of the verb "mull," meaning "to dull, stupefy," or "to grind to a powder, pulverize." He concludes that the American word "mullethead" may derive from a corruption of the English word "mull-head" and that it became linked with the word for the fish "by clang association."

This, of course, still offers no link to hair or haircuts. For this we turn to the highest authority. The *OED* claims that the term mullet, as we understand it, was "apparently coined, and certainly popularized, by the Brooklyn-based hip-hop sensation The Beastie Boys. Their 1994 rap "Mullet Head" made fun of the hairstyle. The next year band member Mike D. discussed the mullet at length in the second issue of the band's magazine, *Grand Royal*: "There's nothing quite as bad as a bad haircut," said Mike D. "And perhaps the worst haircut of all is the cut we call 'The Mullet.'"

The article goes on to lampoon the hairstyle over several pages. Soon after the issue was published, it became popular for fans of the band, and for youth culture in general, to mock the hairstyle. The song itself goes:

> *You've got names like Billy Ray*
> *Now you sing "Hip Hop Hurray"*
> *Put your Oakleys and your stone-wash on*
> *Watching MTV and you mosh on*
> *No. 1 on the side and don't touch the back*
> *No. 6 on the top and don't cut it wack, Jack*

A member of the Beasties' posse, The Captain, wrote in the same *Grand Royal,* "To me, the mullet is as American as pickups with rifle racks, tractor pulls, Wal-Mart, wet T-shirt contests, slapping your girl upside the head with a frying pan and living in the woods."

Just to be sure they are correct in crediting the Beasties with naming the haircut the "mullet," the BBC and the OED have joined forces for a TV series on BBC Two, called *The Wordhunt.* They are looking to trace the origins of words, and concerning the mullet they ask the question, "Did you sport a mullet and did you call it that before the Beastie Boys released their song?" Perhaps their research will lead to a definitive answer on how and when the short-in-front, long-in-back was christened.

In America, the popularity of the mullet reached its peak from about 1985 to 1992. Though popularity waned among the style conscious, there remain many stalwart mullet wearers. Some have sported it continuously since its glory days. Some wear it as an homage to a bygone era or beloved hockey players or movie stars.

Perhaps we should consider the psychological factors that affect the decisions of people to sport the famous, or infamous, mullet. Do they choose the manly-but-feminine cut in response to being raised by an overbearing mother? Do they have repressed androgynous tendencies? Are they just too lazy to change the style? Do they fear change and therefore refuse to move on to a more modern look? Do they think the long-in-the-back look is a way to rebel and stick it to "the man." Are

Like mother, like son.

The sun illuminates a waterfall mullet.

they attempting to hold onto their lost youth? There are, surely, as many answers as there are mullets. Perhaps, someday, the American Medical Association or the American Psychiatric Association will do the research necessary to give a definitive answer. Until then, we can only speculate.

Today, among people in the more conservative "red" states of America, among the youth of Asia and Europe (especially male athletes), and among the suspects on any given episode of the television reality show *Cops*, the mullet thrives. Hockey players and pro wrestlers love the mullet. The mullet is particularly associated with the American working man, fans of country music, and followers of heavy metal rock and roll. Some lesbians with an inclination to dress in a masculine way wear femullets.

Perhaps, like the miniskirt, hot pants, and cocktail music, the mullet will cycle itself around again and have a public resurgence. Have we already seen signs of a slow and stealthy move back into the spotlight for the mullet? There is no doubt that Tom Hanks, the biggest of all

American movie stars, sported a mullet in the 2006 film *The Da Vinci Code*. Duane "Dog" Chapman of the hit reality show *Dog the Bounty Hunter* proudly wears a mullet as he captures criminals. Designers such as Gucci, Gaultier, and Lagerfeld have recently topped their runway models with mullets.

Are these diverse and important trendsetters signaling a new mullet revival by urging us to do the 'do? Is the world ready for the return of the mullet? Perhaps it never really went away. Perhaps it is only in places like Manhattan and Los Angeles that mullet wearer are in short supply. Take a walk around any fairground in Arkansas, Oklahoma, or even Pennsylvania, and you're liable to spot more than just a few mullets. You'll be reminded that the mullet is more than a fad or a trend. It's been around for ages and will be around for generations—as fathers pass the look on to sons, as new fans look back at the 1980s, and as kids take up hockey and soccer.

Chapter Two

Mullet History, Lore, and Legend

 *Sweet Lincoln's mullet!* ""

—Will Ferrell in *Anchorman: The Legend of Ron Burgundy*

One of the mysteries of the Sphinx—is that a mullet?

Historians and beauticians around the world have worked to trace the history of the mullet, a hairstyle which has been around since man learned to use tools and cut hair. As millennia passed, necessity gave way to fashion in hairstyle. Cuts that featured short hair in front and on top and longer hair in back came and went with the times. Though dubbed the mullet only recently, it is worth a lookback at the mullet throughout history.

In all probability, the first mullet wearers were Cro-Magnon men and Neanderthals. These early hominids had no blow dryers or hair gels, or personal hygiene of any kind, for that matter. An argument could be made that prehistoric man didn't choose his hairstyle, but rather that his haircuts, and his version of the mullet, just evolved. The mullet is the hairstyle of inertia. Others might claim that early men relied on the mullet to survive through ice ages and in varying climates. Cutting their hair in front to keep it out of their eyes must have improved their vision, making them better hunters. Flowing locks in back insulated their necks from cold and rain

A medieval mullet.

and snow, perhaps making them warmer and healthier. The truth could be that the mullet was, in fact, an evolutionary improvement for a more modern primate.

Eventually, *homo sapiens*, courtesy of his large and sophisticated brain, became conscious of "style" and haircuts became hairstyles. Primitive civilizations and tribes used hairstyles to identify friend and foe. Images exist of Hittite warriors from 1500 BC wearing a mullet-like cut. Civilizations such as those of the Assyrians and Moabites favored mullets not unlike those of modern times. Egyptian paintings, carvings, and sculptures show mullets perched high on the heads of both men and women (although often these were wigs).

Some mullet zealots speculate that the Great Sphinx itself is sporting a mullet. Even after 4,000 years of erosion by wind and sand, the Sphinx's "haircut" is clearly visible above and behind his shattered visage. Sadly, for those who would like to see the mullet take an exalted place in the pantheon of hair styles, the Sphinx's "mullet" is likely the *nemes*, the Egyptian royal headcloth. Perhaps archaeologists working in the heat of the desert will someday resolve this issue once and for all.

Evidence of the mullet's existence in evolved civilizations can be found in statues and artwork from Greece dating from the sixth century BC. However, mullets were specifically banned from the Roman army in order to eliminate the possibility of an enemy grabbing a hapless soldier's long hair long enough to slit his throat. The Golden Age of Roman civilization may have been the Dark Ages for the mullet. When the Romans conquered Gaul and Britain, they dispatched barbers to cut the hair of the vanquished barbarians. Vikings and Danes still held tight to their mullets, and it's still a popular hairstyle among Scandinavian people. Modern soldiers worldwide are required to have short haircuts. Although this is surely done to promote uniformity among troops, it might also be the modern remnant of a long-ago Roman anti-mullet prejudice.

With the fall of Rome in 476 AD, the Church became the dominant force in Western civilization. Sometime in the seventh century, the Church began compelling monks to shave the tops of their heads, a rite known as tonsure. Was this the beginnings of the skullet, a mullet variety that shows a shiny, bald pate on top and long hair down the back? Maybe so, but proper (secular) mullets were virtually non-existent through the Dark Ages. With the dawn of the Renaissance, art and philosophy rose again, as did the mullet. Prominent leaders chose long hair over short. Countless artists, musicians, explorers, writers—seemingly all those who were influential at the time—embraced the resurgence of creative hairstyles and again the short-in-front and long-in-back style took a place of prominence. Paintings and engravings of fops and dandies—the vainest, most stylized men of their day—depict hair flowing down their exquisite robes.

In the ancient civilizations of China and Japan people wore a variety of hairstyles. Though mullets themselves seem to be have been rare in Asia, in China the *queue* (or cue) was worn by the Manchus of central Manchuria and later the

Forsooth! Shakespeare had a mullet. Or was it a skullet?

The mulleted John Milton.
Paradise found!

Chinese. The style consisted of the hair in front of the head being shaved off above the temples and the rest braided into a long ponytail, or queue. If a ponytail were lost in battle or cut off, the wearer was said to have lost his honor. A similar style was worn in medieval Japan. The mullet probably did not emigrate from Asia, but perhaps its close cousin, the skullet, did.

Seems all the Dutch masters favored the mullet.

As Europeans sailed across the Atlantic and settled in America, they brought their hairstyles with them. Native Americans wore their hair in a variety of ways—depending on the tribe and their geographical location. The Mohawk tribe's style lives on today in the haircut they favored. There is no record, though, of a Mullet tribe. However, as Europeans conquered and colonized, their styles did the same. Nine colonial leaders out of ten either grew their mullets (pulled back in a bow in back, under a tri-cornered hat) or chose powdered wigs in the same style. Ben Franklin, Thomas Jefferson, even George Washington – they all had mullets. (Though Franklin's would be rightly be judged a skullet.) So did the Puritan parsons. So, commonly, did practitioners of law. The custom endures to this day, as judges in Commonwealth nations around the world wear great mullet-like wigs during trials.

In the nineteenth century, the lawlessness of the Wild West and the Native American inclination toward the mullet led to widespread adoption of the hairstyle. (Even the popular coonskin caps of the day were designed to resemble mullets!) In 1845, James K. Polk was sworn in as the eleventh president of the United States, and he is generally regarded as having the most notable mullet of any President of the United States. Born in North Carolina, he served as governor of Tennessee before he became President and was popular throughout the South. Could his greatest legacy as President be a long line of proud mullet wearers in North Carolina, Tennessee, and throughout the South?

With the advent of the camera, the electric light, the movies, and then television, styles and hairstyles became more important as everyone, especially public figures, became more visible than ever before. Clean-cut hairstyles were ubiquitous throughout the first half of the twentieth century as America fought two world wars and soldiers were the idealized version of our citizens. By the late 1950s, the battle between culture and counter-culture began. Crew cuts were still the norm, but "greasers" and beatniks began to rebel against the button-down times. In the 1960s and '70s, revolution was truly in the air. As the revolutionary politics and music and art gained attention, so did revolutionary hair. Afros and sideburns and ponytails became common looks for men.

Judges and barristers in the U.K. could have chosen any wig style, yet they chose the mullet.

Countless Founding Fathers
sported mullets or mullet wigs,
or skullets like Ben Franklin.

Dandies have for centuries
favored mullets.

Still, the mullet stood in the shadows of style—until former Beatle Paul McCartney sported a full shag in 1972. Neil Aspinall, a close friend of Sir Paul and a principal at Apple Records, said at the time that Paul, "regularly referred to his mutated mop-top as 'the Wings of Pegasus' which may have been the inspiration for his post-Beatles band 'Wings.'" As "the cute one" and his band hit the charts and the road, the mullet/shag became all the rage, capturing the hearts (and heads) of young working class Americans as well as fans all over the world. McCartney unleashed the mullet into American and world-wide popular culture. Again, the mullet was on the rise. David Bowie adopted it famously, in his Ziggy Stardust persona, and other rockers joined the fun. The mullet had found its place in the counterculture of the time. Few could imagine, though, that the Golden Age of the Mullet was about to begin.

It wasn't until the 1980s that the mullet became truly mainstream. The hairstyle became de rigeur for athletes, musicians, and actors. The cut's popularity spread rapidly throughout the world. Rock stars sported them on stage all over the world. Country music stars wore them in places like Nashville, Tennessee, and Branson, Missouri. Almost every hockey player in the National Hockey League and throughout the world sported them—as did baseball stars, quarterbacks, and even basketball players. You could not go to a movie without seeing a movie star—mostly men but many women too—wearing the mullet with pride. You could not watch television without finding a cop show, hospital drama, or family sitcom with stars, guests, and extras proving that they were all business in front and a party in the back.

But like many stars and fads that burn white hot, the popularity of the mullet was not to last. After the mullet boom came the mullet bust. The hairstyle went out of fashion even more quickly than it burst onto the scene. Quickly, the cut became an object of ridicule with the style-conscious and mainstream media alike.

Then a curious thing happened. The mullet started becoming popular with people who didn't have them, who would never wear them. These people loved mullets because they could make fun of them, because they could revel in their absurdity. The fascination took on cult status. The mullet became not a hairstyle but a phenomenon. A cottage industry devoted to mulletude sprang up on the Internet. An ironic tribute to mullet madness came with the release of the ultimate movie homage to the mullet, 2001's *Joe Dirt*, starring David Spade. (A key to Joe's character was that his mother covered a hole in her infant son's skull with a mullet wig.) Once high style, then an object of scorn and a symbol of folly for a generation, the mullet has come full circle and gone retro. In accordance with the ironic spirit of our time and our seemingly endless need to recycle culture and fashion, the mullet has become terribly modern. It remains to be seen whether there will be a popular resurgence for the mullet, but if the past is any indication, mullets will always be with us, in one form or another.

A thing of beauty is a joy
forever!

Chapter Three

Famous Mullets

" *Oh, yeah. I'm always bitching about the mullet, but then if they do a story on the mullet and I don't get a mention, then I get mad. I'm like (with mock indignation), 'Wait a minute! It wasn't just Billy Ray Cyrus! I was there too!'* "

—John Stamos

The following notable men (and a few notable women) have sported mullets at various times. By no means complete, these lists are intended to honor just some of those who have made their mark on the world sporting a tennessee tophat.

Thespian Mullets

OPPOSITE: **Kevin Bacon wore something more like a mane than a mullet in his early roles.**

Richard Dean Anderson – MacGyver himself!

Kevin Bacon – Everybody cut footloose (but Kevin wouldn't cut his hair).

Peter Boyle – The former *Young Frankenstein* monster flirted with a skullet on *Everybody Loves Raymond*.

Kirk Cameron – The *Growing Pains* star was a teen heart-throb, perhaps because of his mullet.

George Clooney – The sex symbol favored a long 'do early in his pre-*ER* and movie star days.

Dave Coulier – The *Full House* wiseguy was funny, perhaps because of his mullet.

David Faustino – Young Bud Bundy had a mullet in early episodes and the plots often revolved around his inability to score with girls. (Coincidence or because of the mullet?)

Jane Fonda – A femme fatale and Oscar winner in *Klute* with a femullet.

Michael J. Fox – Sported a mullet to rock out as Joan Jett's brother in the film *Light of Day*.

Dennis Franz – Sipowitz borrowed Gallagher's hairstyle. Result: skullet.

Anthony Geary – Luke from *General Hospital*. Married Laura with a frolet.

Mel Gibson – Before he was controversial, he sported a mullet in the *Lethal Weapon* franchise.

Steve Guttenberg – His mullet was seemingly in every movie made in the '80s!

ABOVE: **David Faustino—Bud Bundy wasn't cool but his hair was.**

RIGHT: **Michael J. Fox and Joan Jett offered us two mullets in the movie *Light of Day*.**

For Mel Gibson, before there was *The Passion of the Christ*, there was his passion for the mullet.

ABOVE: Michael Keaton wore a mullet before his hairline receded.

RIGHT: Before *Baywatch* and his red swim trunks made him world famous, David Hasselhoff was famous for his talking car and his excellent mullet.

OPPOSITE: Steve Guttenberg—sadly, both his career and his great mullet have seemingly vanished.

Corey Haim and Corey Feldman – "The Coreys" shared a name and a haircut.

David Hasselhoff – Drove fast and looked hot in a mullet in *Knight Rider*.

Florence Henderson – Mrs. Brady's classic femullet set a standard.

Howard Hesseman – Dr. Johnny Fever in *WKRP in Cincinnati*.

Ron Jeremy – Porn king. You know what they say, "Big skullet, big…"

Mario Lopez – *Saved by the Bell*, but not by the barber.

Michael Keaton – In *Clean and Sober*.

Nancy McKeon – She was Jo, the smart one, on *The Facts of Life*. Smart enough to sport a femullet.

Richardo Montalban – As Captain Kirk's nemesis, Khan, in *Star Trek II: The Wrath of Khan*, he sported a villanous grey mullet.

Chuck Norris – A man of few words, but mess with Walker's mullet and he'll kick your patoot.

ABOVE: **Nancy McKeon** learned the facts of hair on *The Facts of Life*.

RIGHT: **Chuck Norris**—martial arts expert, movie star—was both *Walker, Texas Ranger* and a mullet wearer.

ABOVE: **John Stamos** was the Olsen twins' favorite uncle in *Full House*, probably because of his mullet.

RIGHT: **Mario Lopez** was *Saved by the Bell* but not by the barber.

OPPOSITE: **Patrick Swayze** was hot and hunky during the *Road House* era, just like his mullet.

Brad Pitt – Sex symbol with a mullet above him and Geena Davis under him in *Thelma and Louise*.

Steven Segal – From *Under Siege* to today.

Homer Simpson – Famous television patriarch, he sometimes sports a mullet in flashbacks.

David Spade – In *Joe Dirt*, his mullet was the key to the character and the movie.

John Stamos – His *Full House* hair was one of the signature mullets of the late '80s.

Patrick Swayze – This icon sported his mullet in hit movies like *Dirty Dancing*, *Road House*, and *Ghost*.

Scott Valentine – Nick, Mallory's boyfriend on *Family Ties*, let his hair do all the talking for him.

OPPOSITE: **Brad Pitt attributes much of his success to his haircut.**

Musical Mullets

Alabama – Just about every member of the band wore a mullet.

Syd Barrett – Mad musical mastermind of Pink Floyd's first record.

Pat Benatar – Hell is for children, and heads are for femullets.

Kurtis Blow – The American rapper sports a mullet.

Michael Bolton – Before he cut off his hair and acknowledged his receding hairline.

Jon Bon Jovi – "Livin' on a Prayer" and livin' with a mullet.

Bono – During the early days of U2, his mullet was centerstage.

David Bowie – Ziggy Stardust's *orange* mullet was as groundbreaking as his music.

James Brown – Late in life, the Godfather of Soul's hair tended more towards mullet than pompadour.

FAR LEFT: **Pat Benatar rocked out like few woman ever have—and was certainly one of the sexiest babes to ever wear a femullet.**

LEFT: **Michael Bolton, like Samson, cut his skullet and cut short his career.**

ABOVE: **Bono—"Unforgettable Fire" and unforgettable hair.**

OPPOSITE: **Jon Bon Jovi favors a mullet to this day.**

David Crosby – In the high times of the 1960s, his skullet was iconic.

Billy Ray Cyrus – The personification of the mullet. With "Achy Breaky Heart," he was huge. Then the world turned against him and his hair. Today, he is back—without the mullet.

Dio – Metal singer.

OPPOSITE: **Billy Ray Cyrus was the King of the Mullet.**

Joe Elliott – Lead singer of rock band Def Leppard.

Mick Fleetwood – Drummer anchoring Fleetwood Mac. Stevie Nicks's hair was more famous, but his skullet was formidable.

Foreigner – The entire original line-up of the band wore a shaggy version of the the mullet.

Kenny G – Clarinet and a permullet.

Daryl Hall – Oates's mustache was more famous but Hall's mullet was also music to our eyes.

James Hetfield – Metallica's frontman sported a mullet from the late '80s to mid '90s.

Michael Jackson – Several plastic surgeries ago, he had a mullet.

Rick James – Superfreak with a Super Permullet.

Joan Jett – She loves rock and roll, and hair all down her neck. A great femullet.

KISS – Under the make up? Mullets!

Lamal – Lead singer of new wave band Kajagoogoo.

Little Richard – Pompadour in the '50s but more recently a mullet. Whoooooo!

Richard Marx – It don't mean nothing without a mullet.

Paul McCartney – From a mop top to a shag to Sir Paul.

Klaus Meine – Lead singer of Scorpions.

George Michael – Mulleted in Wham!

Wolfgang Amadeus Mozart – A mullet wig and a real mullet underneath. Why bother?

OPPOSITE: **Richard Marx lost his mullet and we haven't seen him on MTV since.**

ABOVE: **Paul McCartney's
shag was a touchstone
moment in mullet history.**

OPPOSITE: **Little Richard
evolved from pompadour to
mullet as the years went by.**

Night Ranger – The whole band.

Ric Ocasek – Leader of The Cars. His mullet and his music hooked him a supermodel as a wife.

Ozzy Osbourne – Mulleted as he bit the bird's head off.

Steve Perry – Lead singer of Journey.

Tom Petty – The head Heartbreaker wore it long in back.

OPPOSITE: **Lionel Richie wore the classic jheri curl mullet.**

Poison – Something to believe in? How about a mullet?!

Prince – Purple rain couldn't soak his "Jheri curl" mullet.

Lionel Richie – Fame with The Commodores, greater fame as a mulleted solo singer. (Father of Nicole.)

Quiet Riot – Mullets all around, when they still had all their own hair.

Ricky Skaggs – American country music singer with the courage to wear a mullet.

Spandau Ballet – You know this much is true: they all had mullets!

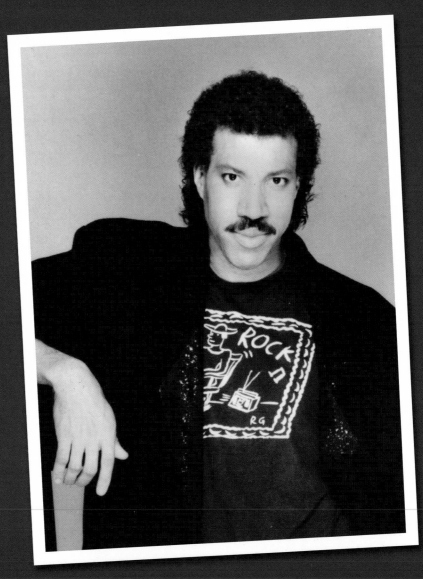

Spinal Tap – The entire band (except for the exploding drummer).

Rick Springfield – Australian musician, heart-throb, and actor pounded out "Jessie's Girl" with a mullet.

Sylvester Stallone – He took on the Russians with a mullet in *Rambo: First Blood Part II*.

Rod Stewart – His was a classic '70s shag mullet. He's been marrying hot babes ever since.

OPPOSITE: **Rod Stewart wooed supermodels and actresses worldwide with his shaggy version of the mullet.**

Randy Travis – American country music singer as sincere as his mullet.

Travis Tritt – Won millions of country fans with his music and his hair.

Van Halen – The entire original band, but did Sammy Hagar have a mullet?

"Weird Al" Yankovic – His Permullet was a parody of itself.

Athletic Mullets

Andre Agassi – Before the tennis champ shaved his head.

Mike Awesome – American professional wrestler—just one of many who love the mullet.

Rod Beck – He had baseball's meanest mullet. May it rest in peace.

David Beckham – Sex symbol and style icon, he has had many hairstyles, but in his early years, his mullet was his favorite.

Larry Bird – One of basketball's greats, he and his hair were the pride of French Lick, Indiana, and the Boston Celtics.

Brian Bosworth – The handsome, blond linebacker for the Oklahoma Sooners seemed destined for stardom, only to have both his acting career and his NFL career sputter out. Perhaps he tried to blame his mullet?

John Daly – Golfer, rebel, mullet wearer.

OPPOSITE: **Andre Agassi, before he shaved his head, wore a dramatic mullet.**

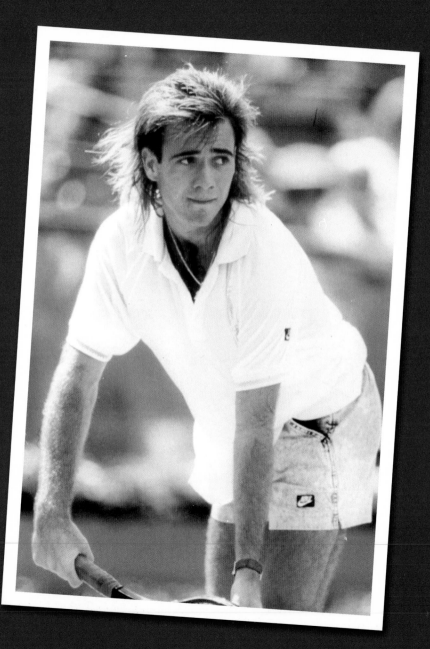

Johnny Damon – He led the Red Sox to a World Series championship on a team of "idiots," and his hair was an icon in Boston.

Dennis Eckersley – Hall of Fame Major League Baseball reliever with a great moustache and mullet.

Brian Engblom – Canadian National Hockey League analyst and former player.

Hulk Hogan – The Hulkster has a skullet—both as a wrestler and now on his reality television show.

Jaromir Jagr – Czech, NHL star, and mullet wearer.

Randy Johnson – American Major League Baseball pitcher. At 6' 10" one the tallest mullet wearers ever!

John Kruk – American Major League Baseball analyst and former player.

Don Mattingly – As captain of the New York Yankees, he was fined and suspended by George Steinbrenner for wearing his hair too long—in a mullet.

Marty McSorley – Retired Canadian National Hockey League player.

Barry Melrose – ESPN National Hockey League analyst and former coach.

Joe Pepitone – The first New York Yankee to bring a blow dryer into the clubhouse.

Mitch Williams – Retired Major League Baseball relief pitcher.

OPPOSITE: **Listen here, Brother! Don't mess with the Hulk's skullet!**

Miscellaneous Mullets

Duane Chapman – Bounty hunter and star of *Dog the Bounty Hunter*, a reality TV series.

David Copperfield – Grandiose magician with a beautiful mullet. (An honorable mention goes to newcomer Criss Angel's frullet.)

Ellen DeGeneres – American comedienne, actress, lesbian, and talk show host.

Fabio – Romance novel model who (in theory) makes the mullet sexy.

TOP: **One of magician David Copperfield's best tricks was getting supermodel Claudia Schiffer to fall in love with him and his mullet.**

RIGHT: **Ellen DeGeneres is a champion of the femullet movement.**

OPPOSITE: **Fabio could have appeared on on the cover of the romance novel *Mullets of Desire*.**

Michael Flatley – The self-appointed Lord of the Dance is also Lord of the Mullet!

Frankenstein's monster – When you're made of sewn-together corpses, you don't get to choose your hairstyle.

Larry Fortensky – After meeting Liz Taylor in re-hab, he became her seventh husband.

Muammar al-Gaddafi – The once-fierce Libyan leader often sported an AK-47 and a mullet.

Gallagher – Made himself famous by smashing fruit in a mullet.

Incredible Hulk – A *green* mullet, no less.

Captain Planet – Making the planet safe for mullets.

Arnold Schwarzenegger – Now a governor, but then a mullet wearer—in both *Conan* movies.

Jerry Seinfeld – Comedian who might ask, "Is my hairdo a mullet if people no longer call it a mullet?"

Tarzan – Apeman? Mulletman!

OPPOSITE: **Long before his reign as Governor of California, Arnold Schwarzenegger wore a mullet as Conan in two hit movies.**

Chapter Four

How to Cut a Mullet

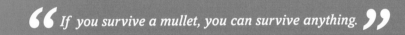 *If you survive a mullet, you can survive anything.*

—George Clooney

Did you know that the city of Gautier, Mississippi, hosts the Gautier Mullet Festival? The annual event includes live bands, a kids' area, and a car show. And although the festival actually celebrates the mullfish called the mullet, in the past the festival's organizers have offered cash prizes for the Best Natural Mullet Haircut, the Best Manmade Mullet Hair-do, a Lifetime Achievement Award, and more. Several other locations throughout the U.S. host their own annual mullet-related festivals.

Want to join the fun and sport a mullet of your own? Here's how. Give the following instructions to the person cutting your hair. (It is doubtful that you can make any use of them yourself, unless you are willing to risk making a complete Hack Job of your head.)

The mullet is two haircuts rolled into one. To achieve the mullet look, the hair is cut shorter on top and left long, perhaps very long, in the back. The hairstyle is great for people with rounder faces, or for those who want to highlight their eyes or cheekbones as a focal feature of their faces. It's also a great style for making the neck look longer.

OPPOSITE: **You won't be alone sporting a mullet at the races.**

To create the style, you will need:

- four butterfly clips
- styling comb
- haircutting scissors

Separate the hair into four sections and secure with the butterfly clips. The top section should be a roughly rectangular section going from the front hairline to the middle of the crown (the middle of the curve at the back of the head) and

"Agent 002, here are the top secret instructions for how to cut a mullet. Do not let it fall into enemy hands."

from the top of the left side to the top of the right. The left and right side sections start at the front hairline on each side and stop just behind the ears. The remaining hair in back should be twisted up and secured with a clip, out of your way.

The Front

The front of the hair is cut as it would be in a clean, traditional man's haircut. Comb the hair forward over the forehead. Cut the bangs to the desired length.

The Sides

Take down one side and comb the hair forward and cut the side guide at an angle using the bang length to guide you. Then comb the hair straight down and carefully cut the hair around the ears. Take vertical slices out of the hair that are about 1/4 inch wide, starting at the front and using your guide cuts to ensure even lengths. Work back along the side in 1/4 inch increments. Repeat these steps on the

High school yearbooks are filled with puka shells and mullets.

opposite side.

Now, return to the top section of the hair and comb the hair upward from both sides so that you are holding the hair in the center of the head from left to right; using your bangs cut as a guide, cut the hair to this length. Work your way back along the top of the head to the end of the section.

Move to either the front or back of the head and comb small segments of the hair from the corners (where the top and sides meet) upward and out at an angle. Cut the corners you see there to blend the top and sides together. This will create a smooth look when finished.

A mullet on the short side with patterned sidebars.

The Back

Take down the back section of the hair and comb it smooth. Comb thin segments (1/4 inch) of the hair in back straight up and hold them with the hair at the rear of the top section of the head. Cut these segments using the top hair as a length guide. Continue combing the segments up and cutting them using the top length guide until all the hair has been cut. Then comb the hair down and cut the bottom hairline to the desired length.

Be sure to blend the rear sides with the back lengths by combing horizontally along the "join" of the side and back sections and cutting away any "corners."

Note: The Flowbee could be the mullet wearer's best friend. This vacuum haircutting system delivers the perfect dome on top to compliment the flowing tresses in the back. Once your mullet is cut, perhaps a Flowbee could be part of your hair maintenance arsenal.

Step aside, we're looking at the cool guy behind you.

Chapter Five

A Field Guide to Mullets

> " *I never actually think, okay, next week I'm going to get a mullet. I just wake up one morning and I'm bored with my hair and shave it off. It's just something I enjoy.* "
>
> —David Beckham

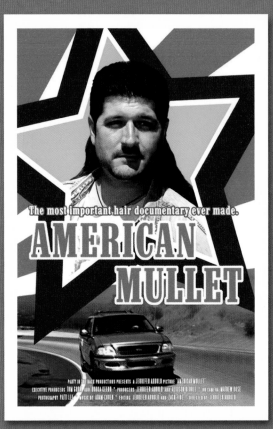

The most important hair documentary ever made.

AMERICAN MULLET

Mullet Movie Alert! Have you seen the documentary *American Mullet* (2001)? Director Jennifer Arnold sets out to explore America by examining the fascination we have with mullets and those that wear them. At once absurd and revealing, it is essential viewing for anyone with a passion for the mullet.

The popularity of mullets has changed with the times. Today, mullets are both loved as a symbol of ironic comedy and as a bold fashion or cultural statement. For lovers and haters of mullets alike, though, it can be thrilling to spot a striking, handsome, absurd, or unique mullet in public. Common at country fairs, NASCAR races, high school football games, and rare in urban settings or black-tie events, a mullet is often the center of everyone's attention. This field guide is dedicated to everyone who now wears, or once wore, a mullet—and to everyone who delights in the grandeur of the hairstyle.

A clown with
a skullet wig.

Creative in every way.

05/01/2006.

A mullet rancher.

A future Locks of Love donor?

A windswept mullet on the plains.

This is a special man with a special haircut.

Another mullet at the track.

A Jackomullet!

A woman and her femullet enjoy Disneyland.

Grey or not, a mullet is still "a party in the back."

A mullet that defies gravity—with the use of the proper product.

Total Baldy McMullet!

A working man getting the job done—with his mullet.

Mullet wearers love any party, especially a wedding.

Mullets are kid's stuff.

This is the handsome ponytail on the back end of a mullet.

Getting ready to take his mullet out on the boat.

A football game is a mullet's natural habitat.

A mullet,
cool shades,
and a babe that
adores you.
Heaven!

Skeet shooting is a sport popular with some mullet wearers.

Sometimes you can't be sure where the mullet ends and the back hair begins.

"Son, one day I'll teach you how to talk to girls, and shave, and take care of your mullet."

Waiting for the show to start, but the party in the back has already begun.

A little color can make the mullet.

After a party, the wearer can tire but rarely will his mullet.

This mullet is truly a party in the back!

Stretch it out from here to Little Rock.

Here the glorious mullet in the background eclipses the photographer's subject.

Nope, not a skullet!

Hot blondes love a guy with a mullet.

A man, his girl, and his mullet at the beach.

A long flowing mullet waiting for a bus.

"Hey, this dude is taking a picture of my mullet! Sweet!"

Children are the future—of the mullet.

Tickets to the game—$25.00
Pretzel—$3.00.
A great mullet—priceless.

Sometimes a mullet just needs some blue on top.

Shades are the right accessory to go with a great mullet.

Nothing is as American as a hot dog and a mullet.

It is said that the coonskin cap resembles a mullet, but usually you can tell the difference.

Getting a new tattoo to go with a classic mullet.

A femullet with a long, beautiful braid.

True love is a couple
that shares everything—
including a hairstyle.

How can it be so straight
on top and so curly in back?
Remarkable.

A distinguished salt and pepper mullet and wire-rimmed glasses make a real statement.

Shaved hair on the side, flowing blond hair in back, and a beer. Classic!

Mulleted chicks need to potty, too!

A good father that loves his son—and his son's mullet.

Mullets are as strong as safety helmets and will suffice in construction areas.

Hoop earrings are a great accessory to the femullet.

The merry-go-round reminds him of his youth, when his mullet was only down to his shoulders

Mullet wearers need vacations, too. Nice braids.

"I need another shell necklace to go with my mullet."

Brides are always beautiful, and so are mullets!

The braided ponytail can make a mullet special.

If mullets were gold, the track would be Fort Knox.

Keep your arms, legs, and mullets in the car at all times!

A big man with a big mullet.

"Look at the bald guy on TV!"

A night on the town can can take a lot out of you, but a mullet can party all night.

Chapter Six

A Handy Mullet Reference Guide

" I bumped into the fashion industry in a rock 'n' roll band, and I wasn't very fashionable, really... I'm the man who brought you the mullet. "

—Bono

Did you know? There are at least twenty-seven places in the world that have "mullet" in their names—from Mullet Creek in New South Wales to Mullet, Albania, to Mullet Hall Plantation on Johns Island, South Carolina. Simon Varwell, of Glasgow, has made it his mission in life to visit all of these sites and perhaps to discover some more. So far? Eight. (Some certainly named after people.)

Mullet Varieties and Terminology

OPPOSITE: **A side view of a classic mullet.**

Here is a short list of the terminology used in talking about mullets and some of the mullet varieties—both popular and unpopular.

Baldy McMullet

A mullet with very little or no hair in the front or on the sides.

Bowlet

Like a bowl haircut, but with a party around back!

The Business Mullet

Exemplifies, literally, the spirit of the mullet motto, "business up front and a party in the back." Wearers of this style are trying to fit into the corporate scene and often braid their mullet or tuck it into a ponytail.

Chullet

A mullet sported by a child.

Curllet

A mullet featuring long curly hair cascading down the wearer's neck.

De-mullification

The process of removing one's mullet, it can be traumatic for the long-term mullet wearer.

Euromullet

A mullet worn by a European. To Americans, this mullet often appears suaver and more sophisticated than its domestic cousins. Or more pretentious.

ABOVE: **Baldy McMullet.**

RIGHT: **Baldy McMullet with a braided ponytail.**

ABOVE: A mulleted business-man, taking care of business.

RIGHT: A curllet.

The Feather Mullet

Short and spiky on top and long and luxurious out back. Women often choose this mullet style.

Femullet

A mullet worn by a female, it can be worn by women in any walk of life. The two most famous are probably Joan Jett's rock-and-roll mullet and Florence Henderson's Carol Brady mullet. (Also see *shmullet*.)

Frolet

This extremely rare, but not unheard-of, combination of a mullet and an Afro can be stylish or foolish.

Frullet

A reversed variation of the mullet (derived from "front mullet"), where the hair on the back of the head is cut short, leaving a long fringe hanging over the face in front. During the '80s, this hair style was popular among skateboarding teens—think Edward Furlong in *Terminator 2*.

"Weird Al" has been rockin' the frollet since his *UHF* days.

The Jedi Mullet

From Mark Hamill's Luke Skywalker to Ewan Mc-
Gregor's Obi-Wan, George Lucas's fictional galaxy
seems to be full of mullets.

Jheri Curl

The result when people with naturally curly hair apply
Jheri curl treatments to their hair make the curls big-
ger and to keep them in place. Lionel Richie sported
such a mullet.

Meximullet

A mullet worn by a Mexican. (See also *Mulletino.*)

Mullestache

A moustache worn with a mullets, common in the
Golden Age of Mullets. (See Hall of Fame pitcher Dennis Eckersley.)

Mullet

The classic haircut that says, "Business in the front,
and a party in the back."

LEFT: **Mullets come from all over the world.**

RIGHT: **A feather mullet.**

Mulleteer

Someone who proudly sports a mullet.

Mulletagus

Scientific name for "Mulletese Twins"—a rare instance of Siamese twins conjoined at the mullet. (No known photographs exist.)

Mullet Chan

A mullet worn by those of Chinese descent.

Mulletino

A mullet worn by a Mexican. (See also *Meximullet*.)

Mullet Masztalerz

A mullet worn by those of Polish descent.

Mullet Singh

A mullet worn by those of Indian descent.

Mullestache

A mullet and moustache worn together.

OPPOSITE: **Two hair-dos in one— "The jellyfish mullet."**

Mulleteer

A nickname for a young mullet wearer, à la "muske-teer."

Mulletude

The attitude common to those whose heads are adorned with mullets.

Mullhawk

A mullet combined with a mohawk.

Perllet

A permed mullet, also referred to as a permullet. Also includes crimped mullets.

The Rattail Mullet

A mullet with a long tail sprouting from the back.

Shmullet

Also known as a She-Mullet, a mullet worn by a fe-male. (See femullet.)

ABOVE: A young muleteer.

RIGHT: A Mullet Singh.

Skmullet

The all-too-common style that's balding on top with a comb-over, long in the back.

Skullet

A mullet that is bald on the top with a normal mullet in back, usually due to premature balding. (See Hulk Hogan.)

Stingray

A mullet style bordering on a "tail," where the hair in back is long, straight, and tapered, much like the tail of the stingray.

Tropical Mullet

A cross between Rasta dreadlocks and a mullet. Also knows as a rastamullet.

ABOVE: **Some mullets defy proper categorization.**

OPPOSITE: **A Rastamullet—very rare and very handsome.**

The Mullet Atlas

Here is a short guide to the mullet in various languages and cultures around the world. Some would argue that the modern mullet, like movies or democracy, is an American export, but perhaps, like so much of what makes America special, the mullet to us came through Ellis Island and only later became native. Regardless of whence the mullet came, we do know that virtually every spot on earth has come up with its own name for the style.

	Argentina	Cubana, colectivero
	Australia	Freddie Firedrill
	Austria	Gnackmatten ("nape rug").
	Bosnia	fudbalerka ("footballer")
	Brazil	Chitãozinho e Xororó
	Canada	coupe Longueuil (French Canadian), pad (English Canadian)
	Chile	chocopanda, chocola, or simply "choco"

Colombia	greña paisa, siete (seven)	
Croatia	fudbalerka ("footballer hair")	
Czechoslavakia	olek ("newt")	
Denmark	Bundesliga-hår (football league hair), svenskerhår (Swede-hair), hockeyhår, or nakkegarn ("yarn by the back of the neck")	
Finland	takatukka ("rear hair"). Also lätkätukka ("ice hockey haircut") or tsekkitukka ("Czech hair")	
France	coupe à la Waddle (after footballer Chris Waddle). Also can be referred to as "nuque longue," signifying long hair on the back of the neck.	
Germany	Vokuhila, meaning "vorne kurz, hinten lang" (short in the front, long in the back). Also Ossispoiler ("aerodynamic device").	

	Greece	Χαίτη (Hety) or Λασπωτήρας (Laspotiras) which means ("mud-flap")
	Guam	chad
	Hungray	focistafrizura, or Bundesliga ("soccer player hair")
	Iceland	Hebbi (referring to Icelandic singer Herbert Guðmundsson who sported the hairstyle), or sítt að aftan ("long in the back")
	Israel	vilon (meaning "curtain.")
	Italy	capelli alla tedesca ("hair at German style"). Also referred to as alla McGyver, sette (seven, referring to the hairstyle's shape), or codino (little tail)
	Japan	urufu hea ("wolf hair")
	Macedonia	"џигерица" [dzigerica] (meaning the "liver haircut.")
	The Netherlands	matje ("little carpet/mat"), Duitse mat (German mat)

Norway	hockeysveis, meaning "hockey hairstyle"	
Poland	Czeski piłkarz ("Czech football player"), dywan ("carpet"), or plereza ("cover the back")	
Portugal	XF (refers to a popular motorcycle model), or semi reboque (which means a big truck trailer). They also use the words Deixe Ficar which is short for deixe ficar atrás (what you say to your hairdresser when you want him not to cut the hair on the back of your head).	
Puerto Rico	playero ("beachcomber" or "beach style" to reflect its popularity among surfers)	
Romania	chic ("long hair at the neck")	
Sanskrit	sikha ("crest" or "top-knot"). The Hindu wearing a top knot can let it go bushy and voila, a mullet.	

Serbia Tarzanka (obvious reference to Tarzan the Ape Man.) Another term is Krčedinka, referring to the mullet's popularity in the village of Krčedin.

Slovenia Bundesliga or simply metlica ("a small broom")

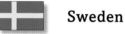 **Spain** No exact translation equivalent, although the term la capa ("the cape") is often used, as well as El Corte MacGyver

 Sweden hockeyfrilla ("ice hockey haircut").

Turkey Aslan yelesi ("lion's mane") or Fikirtepe modeli (referring to Fikirtepe, a suburb of Istanbul where this style is popular).

Mullet Bay Park—a popular
vacation destination for
someone with the right hair.

A mulleted Adonis and family.

Mullet Synonyms

Here are some terms that that can be used interchange-
ably to describe the classic mullet. They are almost as creative
as the hairstyle itself.

- **7 (the shape of a mullet)**
- **10-90 (10% on top, 90% in the back)**
- **Achy-Breaky-Bad-Mistakey**
- **Alabama Waterfall**
- **All Porch, No Awning**
- **Ape-Drape**
- **B&T (bridge and tunnel)**
- **Backpack**
- **Beaver Paddle**
- **Beaver Tail**

- Bi-level
- The Billy Ray
- Boz (after Brian Bosworth!)
- Business in the Front, Party in the Back
- Camaro Crash Helmet
- Camaro cut
- Canadian Passport
- Coupe Longueuil
- Either/Or
- El Camino
- Guido
- Hack Job
- Hockey Hair

- **IROC Cut**
- **The Joe Dirt**
- **Kentucky Waterfall**
- **Lobster Mudflap**
- **Long Island Iced Tease**
- **Louisiana Purchase**
- **The LPGA**
- **The MacGyver**
- **Mississippi Mudflap**
- **Missouri Compromise**
- **Mudflap**
- **Nebraska Neckwarmer**
- **Neck Blanket**
- **Ranchero**

Richard Dean Anderson could fix anything as MacGyver, even his hair.

- River Cut (as in Colorado)
- SFLB (short in front, long in back)
- STLB (short top, long back)
- S&L Crisis
- Safety Cut
- Shag
- Shlong (short long)
- Short-Long (or Sho-lo for short)
- Shortly Longback
- Soccer Rocker
- Sphinx
- Squirrel Pelt
- Tennessee Tophat

- **Texas Tailgate**
- **The Wrestlemania**
- **Wrestler's Wig**
- **Yep-Nope**
- **Ziggy Stardust**

David Bowie broke new ground in rock and roll, and hairstyles, as Ziggy Stardust.

Your Mullet Photos Here

Back light, red lights an' strobe lights too,
Were all the rage for me an' you
Only one thing I miss more than that:
I want my mullet back

—Billy Ray Cyrus, "I Want My Mullet Back"